ADVANTAGE OF BEING SINGLE

BEING SINGLE CAN OFFER YOU THE FREEDOM TO MAKE YOUR OWN DECISIONS, FOCUS ON PERSONAL GROWTH. AND PURSUE YOUR OWN INTERESTS WITHOUT THE RESPONSIBILITIES AND COMPROMISES THAT COME WITH BEING IN A RELATI

NILABHRU DAS

Made with ♥ on the Notion Press Platform
www.notionpress.com

Introduction:

Chapter 1: Independence and Freedom

Chapter 2: Financial Stability

Chapter 3: Stronger Social Connections

Chapter 4: Personal Growth and Self-Discovery

Chapter 5: More Time and Energy for Personal Pursuits

Chapter 6: The Power of Alone Time

Conclusion:

Introduction

Being single is often portrayed in a negative light in our society, with many people feeling like they need to be in a relationship to be happy or fulfilled. But the truth is, being single can be a wonderful and fulfilling experience, and there are many benefits to being unattached.

Firstly, one of the biggest advantages of being single is independence and freedom. When you're not in a relationship, you have the freedom to make decisions and act independently. You don't have to worry about the needs or wants of a partner, and you can make choices based solely on your own desires. This can lead to a greater sense of autonomy and confidence, as you learn to trust your own instincts and make choices that feel right for you.

Another advantage of being single is financial stability. When you're not in a relationship, you don't have to worry about splitting expenses or sharing finances with another person. This means you have more control over your money and can make decisions based solely on your own financial goals and needs. You can save more money, invest in your future, and make choices that will benefit you in the long run.

Also, being single can result in more solidified social ties. You have more time and energy to invest in your friendships and family ties when you're not in a romantic relationship. Being able to spend more time with the people that matter to you can result in deeper and more meaningful social interactions.

Another advantage of being single is personal growth and self-discovery. When you're not in a relationship, you have the freedom to pursue personal growth without the constraints of a romantic partner. This can lead to a greater sense of self-awareness and a better understanding of yourself. You can explore your own interests, hobbies, and passions, and learn more about what makes you happy and fulfilled.

Also, being single can provide you more time and energy to pursue your interests. You have greater control over how you spend your time and energy while you're single. As a result, you will have more time to focus on your objectives and interests outside of work and school. Without the restrictions of a love partner, you are free to follow your own goals.

Finally, being single can be a wonderful opportunity to enjoy alone time and solitude. When you're not in a relationship, you have the opportunity to recharge and reflect without the distractions of a romantic partner. This can lead to a greater appreciation for the benefits of alone time, and a deeper understanding of your own needs and desires.

In conclusion, being single can be a wonderful and fulfilling experience. There are many benefits to being unattached, including independence and freedom, financial stability, stronger social connections, personal growth and self-discovery, more time and energy for personal pursuits, and the power of alone time. If you're currently single, I encourage you to embrace and celebrate the joys of solitude, and to appreciate all the wonderful things that come with being unattached. an exploration of the many ways in which being single can be a fulfilling and rewarding experience.

Chapter 1

Independence and Freedom

When you're single, you have the freedom to make choices based solely on your own desires and needs. You don't have to worry about the needs or wants of a partner, and you can make choices without worrying about how they will affect someone else. This can lead to a greater sense of autonomy and confidence, as you learn to trust your own instincts and make choices that feel right for you.

One of the most empowering things about being able to make decisions and act independently is the ability to pursue your own goals and aspirations. When you're not in a relationship, you have the freedom to focus on your own career, education, or personal hobbies and interests. You can make choices that are solely focused on your own growth and development, without worrying about how they will impact a partner.

Another benefit of being able to make decisions and act independently is the ability to take risks and try new things. When you're not in a relationship, you have the freedom to explore your own interests and passions and to take risks without worrying about how they will affect someone else. You can try new things, make mistakes, and learn from your experiences, all without the fear of letting someone else down.

A stronger sense of self-awareness and self-discovery might result from being able to decide for oneself and take autonomous action. You may completely explore your own preferences and desires when you are free to make decisions without having to consider a partner's demands or goals. You can discover more about who you are, your likes and dislikes, and the things that make you happy and fulfilled.

Of course, being able to make decisions and act independently isn't always easy. Sometimes, it can be challenging to make choices without the input or support of a partner. But ultimately, the ability to make decisions and act independently is a wonderful gift that can lead to greater personal growth and fulfillment.

So, if you're currently single, I encourage you to embrace the joys of being able to make decisions and act independently. Take advantage of the freedom and autonomy that comes with being unattached and use it as an opportunity to explore your own interests, passions, and goals. And if you're not single, remember that everyone deserves the freedom to make choices and act independently, and try to support and encourage your partner's autonomy whenever possible.

When you're not in a relationship, you have the freedom to make choices that are solely based on your own desires and needs. You can pursue your own interests and passions, without worrying about how they will impact a partner. This can lead to a greater sense of autonomy and confidence, as you learn to trust your own instincts and make choices that feel right for you.

One of the biggest benefits of being single is the freedom to make your own schedule. You can plan your days and nights however you like, without having to consult with a partner. This can lead to a greater sense of control over your life, as you can prioritize your own needs and interests.

Also, being single gives you more freedom in your daily life. You don't need to plan your trip around your partner's schedule; you can go whenever you like. You don't have to be concerned about how new endeavors or employment will affect others when you take them on. You are free to make impulsive plans and decisions without having to consider how they will fit into the life of your partner.

Another benefit of being single is the freedom to choose your own living situation. You can live wherever you want, without having to worry about a partner's preferences or needs. You can choose to live alone, with roommates, or with family and friends, depending on what feels right for you.

Of course, being single isn't always easy. Sometimes, it can be lonely or isolating, and it can be challenging to make all your own decisions without the input or support of a partner. But ultimately, the freedom and flexibility that comes with being single is a wonderful gift that can lead to greater personal growth and fulfilment.

So, if you're currently single, I encourage you to embrace the freedom and flexibility that comes with being unattached. Take advantage of the ability to make your own choices and live life on your own terms. And if you're not single, remember that everyone deserves the freedom and flexibility to pursue their own interests and passions, and try to support and encourage your partner's autonomy whenever possible.

When you are single, you have a lot of free time and flexibility to pursue your interests and passions. This can be incredibly rewarding and fulfilling, and it can have many positive effects on your life. Here are some of the benefits of pursuing personal goals and hobbies when you are single:

You can focus on yourself: When you are in a relationship, you often have to compromise and consider your partner's needs and desires. While this is a natural and healthy part of a relationship, it can sometimes mean that you must put your own goals and aspirations on hold. When you are single, you have the freedom to focus entirely on yourself and your own growth.

You can discover new interests: When you have more free time and space to explore, you may discover new hobbies and interests that you never knew you had. This can be incredibly exciting and fulfilling, and it can help you develop new skills and passions that will enrich your life in many ways.

You may boost your self-esteem and confidence by pursuing your interests and personal goals. You will experience a sense of pride and accomplishment as you discover new things and reach your objectives, which will increase your confidence and help you feel more capable and self-assured.

You can meet new people: Pursuing personal goals and hobbies can also be a great way to meet new people and expand your social circle. Whether you join a club, take a class, or attend an event, you will have the opportunity to connect with like-minded people who share your interests and passions.

Pursuing personal objectives and interests can be a terrific way to decompress after a hard day or week and alleviate stress. Whether you like to draw, hike, or make music, engaging in activities that you love can help you relax and recharge, leaving you feeling refreshed and energized.

In conclusion, being able to pursue personal goals and hobbies when you are single can have many positive effects on your life. Whether you want to focus on your own growth and development, discover new interests, build confidence, meet new people, or reduce stress, pursuing personal goals and hobbies can help you achieve your goals and lead a more fulfilling life. So, if you are single,

Don't hesitate to take advantage of this time to explore your interests and passions. You never know what amazing opportunities and experiences may be waiting for you. Thanks for reading, and I'll see you next time.

Chapter 2

Financial Stability

Let's talk about the obvious: you don't have to spend money on another person. When you're single, you're only responsible for your own expenses. You don't have to worry about buying gifts for birthdays, anniversaries, or Valentine's Day. You don't have to spend money on dates or vacations for two people. You don't have to worry about paying for a larger living space to accommodate a partner. All of these expenses can add up quickly, and being single means that you get to keep that money in your own pocket.

In addition to the direct financial benefits of being single, there are also indirect benefits that can help you save money. For example, when you're single, you have more flexibility in terms of where you live and work. You don't have to worry about a partner's job or commute, which means that you can live in a more affordable area or take a job that pays less but is more fulfilling. You can also take advantage of opportunities to travel or relocate without worrying about how it will affect your partner's life and career.

Another advantage of being single is that you have more control over your own finances. When you're in a relationship, it's common to share financial responsibilities, such as joint bank accounts or credit cards. While this can be helpful in some ways, it can also make it harder to manage your own money. When you're single, you have the freedom to create a budget and stick to it without worrying about anyone else's spending habits. You can save money for your own goals, such as buying a house or starting a business, without having to compromise with a partner.

Finally, being single can also be an opportunity to focus on your career and build your wealth. When you don't have the responsibilities of a relationship, you can dedicate more time and energy to your work. You can take on extra projects or work longer hours without worrying about how it will affect your partner's life. This can help you earn more money, advance in your career, and build your savings.

Of course, being single isn't always easy, and there are certainly emotional and social challenges that come with it. But from a purely economic standpoint, there are many advantages to being single that should be celebrated. So, whether you're single by choice or circumstance, take advantage of the financial benefits and use them to build the life and future that you want.

Hey everyone, welcome back to my vlog. Today we're going to talk about how being single can lead to greater financial stability and security.

As someone who's been single for a while, I've realized that there are many financial benefits to being on your own. Here are some of the key reasons why:

First off, you have total control over your finances when you're single. You don't need to be concerned about another person's spending patterns or financial objectives. You have the power to make financial decisions that are in your best interests and consistent with your values and aspirations.

This means that you can save more money, invest in your future, and make financial decisions that will benefit you in the long run. For example, if you want to save up for a down payment on a house or start investing in the stock market, you can do so without having to consult with a partner or worry about how it might affect them.

Second, not having a partner frees you from having to share your money. If you have high-paying work or are able to save a sizeable amount of your salary, this might be a tremendous financial advantage.

When you're single, you can use your income to build up your savings, pay off debt, or invest in your future. You don't have to worry about supporting another person financially, which can be a significant expense.

Thirdly, living expenses may be reduced as a result of being single. When you live alone, you are free from the burden of paying someone else's share of the rent, electricity, or groceries. If you reside in a high-priced location or prefer a compact home, this may be extremely advantageous.

Additionally, being single means that you have more flexibility when it comes to your living situation. You can choose to live in a cheaper area or in a smaller space, which can help you save money on rent and other expenses.

Finally, being single can lead to greater career opportunities and financial success. When you don't have to worry about another person's needs or career goals, you can focus more on your own career and professional development.

This can lead to higher-paying job opportunities, promotions, and other career advancements. Additionally, being single means that you can be more mobile and flexible when it comes to your career, which can open up even more opportunities for financial success.

In conclusion, being single can lead to greater financial stability and security. When you're on your own, you have more control over your finances, you don't have to split your income with anyone else, you can save money on living expenses, and you have more opportunities for career advancement and financial success.

Of course, being in a relationship can also have its financial benefits, but it's important to recognize that being single can be a positive thing when it comes to your finances. So, if you're currently single, embrace it and take advantage of all the financial benefits that come with it!

Chapter 3

Stronger Social Connections

Being single does not require you to feel lonely, and it does not preclude you from developing enduring bonds with the people in your life. In fact, I would contend that since you don't have the added duties and obligations that being in a romantic relationship might bring, being single may actually allow you more time and energy to devote to these relationships.

So, how can you go about cultivating these relationships? Here are a few tips that I've found helpful.

Firstly, prioritize your friendships. Just because you're not in a romantic relationship doesn't mean that you don't need human connection. Friends can be an incredibly important source of support and can provide a sense of belonging and community that is vital to our well-being. So, make sure that you're actively investing in your friendships. This might mean scheduling regular catchups or phone calls or even just sending a quick text message to check in and see how someone is doing.

Secondly, don't be afraid to be vulnerable with your friends and family. One of the things that can make relationships truly meaningful is the ability to share our thoughts, feelings, and experiences with others in a way that is authentic and vulnerable. When we allow ourselves to be vulnerable to the people in our lives, we create space for deeper connection and understanding. So, if there's something that you're struggling with or that you're excited about, don't be afraid to share it with your friends and family.

Thirdly, be present and engaged when you're spending time with others. In today's world of constant distractions and multitasking, it can be all too easy to be physically present but mentally checked out when we're spending time with others. But if you want to cultivate meaningful relationships, it's important to be fully present and engaged when you're spending time with the people in your life. Put away your phone, give your full attention to the person you're with, and really listen to what they have to say.

Finally, be open to new experiences and new people. Sometimes, we can get stuck in a rut when it comes to our social lives and find ourselves spending time with the same people doing the same things repeatedly. But if we want to cultivate meaningful relationships, it's important to be open to new experiences and new people. Try joining a new club or group, or attending events or activities that interest you. You never know who you might meet or what new connections you might form.

One of the great things about being single is that you have the freedom to meet and connect with a wide variety of people. Whether it's through work, hobbies, or social events, you have the ability to build relationships with people from all walks of life. Here are a few reasons why this can be so beneficial.

Firstly, connecting with a wider range of people can broaden your horizons and expand your worldview. When we spend time with people who have different perspectives and experiences than our own, we are exposed to new ideas and ways of thinking. This can help us to grow and develop as individuals, and can even challenge our existing beliefs and assumptions.

Secondly, connecting with a wider range of people can help us to build empathy and understanding. When we take the time to really get to know someone, we are more likely to see things from their perspective and develop a deeper sense of empathy and understanding for their experiences. This can be especially important in today's world, where there is so much polarization and division.

Thirdly, connecting with a wider range of people can help us to build a more diverse and supportive social network. When we have a wide variety of people in our lives, we are more likely to have a support system that can help us through difficult times. This can be especially important when we are going through periods of change or transition, such as a career change, a move to a new city, or a breakup.

Finally, connecting with a wider range of people can be a lot of fun! When we spend time with people who have different interests and backgrounds than our own, we have the opportunity to try new things and have new experiences. This can be a great way to break out of our comfort zones and explore new parts of ourselves.

So, how can you go about connecting with a wider range of people when you are in single life? Here are a few tips that I've found helpful:

Be open-minded and curious. When you meet new people, approach them with a sense of curiosity and openness. Ask questions about their lives and experiences, and be willing to listen and learn.

Pursue your interests. One of the best ways to meet new people is to get involved in activities and hobbies that interest you. Whether it's joining a sports team, volunteering for a cause you care about, or taking a class, pursuing your interests can help you to connect with like-minded people.

Attend social events. Whether it's a party, a networking event, or a community gathering, attending social events can be a great way to meet new people and expand your social circle.

Use social media. Social media can be a great way to connect with people who share your interests or who are part of your community. Consider joining Facebook groups or following Instagram accounts related to your hobbies or interests.

Many people view being single as a negative aspect of their lives. However, being single can actually have a lot of benefits, including the potential for more meaningful social connections. When you are single, you have more time and energy to invest in your friendships and relationships with family members.

One of the biggest advantages of being single is having the freedom to explore new social circles. When you are in a relationship, it can be easy to become isolated from the rest of the world. However, when you are single, you have the opportunity to meet new people and form deeper connections with those around you.

Being single also allows you to be more intentional about the relationships you cultivate. Instead of settling for a partner who may not be the best fit for you, you can take the time to really get to know the people in your life and focus on building stronger connections with them.

Another benefit of being single is that it allows you to prioritize your own personal growth and development. When you are in a relationship, it can be easy to get caught up in your partner's needs and desires, often at the expense of your own. However, when you are single, you have the space and time to focus on yourself and your own goals, which can lead to a greater sense of fulfilment and purpose.

Being single also allows you to be more present in your relationships with others. When you are not distracted by the demands of a romantic partner, you can fully engage with the people in your life and show up for them in a more meaningful way. This can lead to deeper and more fulfilling social connections that are based on mutual respect, understanding, and support.

Finally, being single can help you develop a stronger sense of self and a greater understanding of your own needs and desires. When you are not defined by a romantic relationship, you are free to explore who you are and what you truly want out of life. This self-awareness can help you form deeper and more authentic connections with others, as you are better able to communicate your own needs and boundaries.

Chapter 4

Personal Growth and Self-Discovery

When you see couples around you or are frequently asked why you are still single, being single might occasionally seem like a curse. Yet I'm here to tell you that living alone can actually present a lot of room for development and self-discovery. Here are a few ways that being single might aid in personal development.

Finding your own identity One of the benefits of being single is that you have the time and space to explore who you are as an individual.

When you're in a relationship, you tend to define yourself in relation to your partner, which can sometimes make it hard to figure out who you are outside of the relationship. Being single allows you to explore your own interests, hobbies, and goals without having to compromise with anyone else. You can spend time figuring out what truly makes you happy and fulfilled, and this can help you develop a stronger sense of self-identity.

Developing independence can also help you develop your independence. When you're in a relationship, you often rely on your partner for emotional and practical support. However, when you're single, you have to learn to rely on yourself. This can be a scary and daunting prospect, but it can also be incredibly empowering. When you learn to take care of yourself and solve problems on your own, you develop a sense of self-sufficiency that can help you in all areas of your life.

Strengthening friendships, Also, being single can free up more time and resources for you to invest in your connections. When you're in a relationship, it's simple to put your relationship over your friendships. On the other hand, being single gives you more time to nurture your friendships and forge closer bonds with the people in your life. This has the potential to be tremendously rewarding and can aid in the development of a solid support system that will be there for you at all times.

Discovering your priorities when you're single, you have the opportunity to really think about what you want out of life. You can take the time to reflect on your values, your goals, and your priorities, and this can help you make decisions that align with your true desires. This can help you avoid getting swept up in relationships that aren't right for you, and it can help you build a life that truly fulfils you.

Developing resilience, Finally, being single can help you develop resilience. When you're single, you have to deal with the ups and downs of life on your own. You may experience rejection, heartbreak, and disappointment, but these experiences can also make you stronger and more resilient. When you learn to pick yourself up after setbacks and keep moving forward, you develop a sense of inner strength that can help you in all areas of your life.

When we are in a relationship, it's easy to get caught up in our partner's wants and needs, often putting our own needs and desires on the back burner. Being single can give us the opportunity to focus on ourselves and to explore who we are on a deeper level. Here are some ways that being single can lead to greater self-awareness and understanding.

Self-reflection, when we are single, we have more time to reflect on our thoughts, feelings, and behaviours. We can ask ourselves questions such as "What do I want out of life?" or "What are my core values?" and really take the time to think about our answers. This self-reflection can help us gain insight into our inner selves and understand what truly matters to us.

Embracing solitude, we may have the chance to enjoy isolation when we are single. Spending time alone may be quite useful for our mental and emotional welfare, even though it can first seem uncomfortable. It enables us to refuel, be in the present, and comprehend our own ideas and feelings on a deeper level.

Pursuing passions When we are single, we have the freedom to pursue our passions without having to consider someone else's wants and needs. We can take a class, travel, or volunteer without having to ask for someone else's permission or worry about how our choices will affect someone else. Pursuing our passions can help us gain a sense of purpose and fulfilment and can also help us understand what truly makes us happy.

Learning from past relationships, Being single can also give us the opportunity to reflect on past relationships and learn from them. We can ask ourselves questions such as "What patterns have I noticed in my relationships?" or "What did I learn from my past breakups?" By reflecting on our past experiences, we can gain insight into our own behaviours and preferences and can use this knowledge to make better choices in future relationships.

Developing self-compassion, and being single can help us develop self-compassion. When we are in a relationship, it's easy to get caught up in our partner's criticisms and judgments and to start to believe that we are not good enough. Being single can give us the opportunity to develop a kinder, more compassionate relationship with ourselves. We can learn to treat ourselves with the same kindness and understanding that we would give to a friend.

While being in a romantic relationship can be wonderful, it can also come with its own set of challenges. When we are in a relationship, we often have to consider our partner's wants and needs, which can sometimes conflict with our own desires for personal growth and self-improvement. Here are some ways that being single can give us the freedom to pursue personal growth without the constraints of a romantic relationship.

When we are single, we have more time to focus on our personal growth and self-improvement. We can take the time to learn new skills, pursue hobbies, and work on personal projects without having to worry about how our choices will affect someone else. This can be incredibly empowering and can help us become the best version of ourselves.

Flexibility in life choices, being single also gives us the flexibility to make life choices that align with our personal goals and values. We can choose to travel, move to a new city, or pursue a new career path without having to consider how these choices will affect someone else. This can be incredibly liberating and can help us make choices that are truly in our best interests.

When we are single, we have more time to focus on our mental and emotional health. We can take the time to prioritize self-care activities such as meditation, therapy, or exercise without having to worry about how these activities will fit into our partner's schedule. This can be incredibly important for our overall well-being and can help us become more resilient and emotionally healthy.

The ability to form deeper friendships can also give us the opportunity to form deeper, more meaningful friendships. When we are in a relationship, it's easy to rely solely on our partner for emotional support, which can sometimes be a burden on the relationship. When we are single, we have more time and energy to form deep connections with friends and family members, which can provide us with a sense of community and belonging.

Development of independence and self-reliance Finally, being single can help us develop a sense of independence and self-reliance. When we are in a relationship, it's easy to become dependent on our partner for certain tasks or decisions. Being single can give us the opportunity to learn how to take care of ourselves and to rely on our own judgment and decision-making skills. This can be incredibly empowering and can help us become more confident and self-assured.

Chapter 5

More Time & Energy for Personal Pursuits

When we are in a relationship, we often have to consider the wants and needs of our partner, which can sometimes limit the amount of time and energy we must pursue our own interests. However, being single can provide us with the freedom and flexibility to focus on the things that we are passionate about. Here are some ways that being single can give us more time and energy to pursue personal interests:

More free time:

When we are single, we have more free time to dedicate to our personal interests. We don't have to worry about scheduling date nights or spending time with our partner's family and friends. This can give us the opportunity to focus on hobbies, creative pursuits, or personal projects that we may not have had time for while in a relationship.

Ability to prioritize:

Being single also gives us the ability to prioritize our personal interests without feeling guilty or selfish. We can spend time doing the things that we love without having to consider how our choices will affect someone else. This can be incredibly empowering and can help us feel more in control of our lives.

More energy:

When we are in a relationship, we may find ourselves constantly giving our energy to our partner and the relationship. Being single can give us the opportunity to focus that energy on ourselves and our personal interests. This can help us feel more fulfilled and energized, which can have a positive impact on all areas of our lives.

Personal growth:

Pursuing personal interests can also be a form of personal growth. When we take the time to focus on our passions and hobbies, we can learn new skills, build confidence, and develop a greater sense of self-awareness. This can help us become the best version of ourselves and can have a positive impact on our relationships and our lives in general.

Opportunities for socialization:

When we pursue our personal interests, we also have the opportunity to connect with others who share similar passions. This can provide us with a sense of community and belonging, which can be incredibly important for our overall well-being. Being single can give us the freedom to explore these social opportunities without having to worry about how our partner will feel.

Autonomy is defined as the freedom to make decisions and act on them independently. When we have a greater sense of autonomy over our time and energy, we have more control over how we live our lives and how we allocate our resources. Here are some of the benefits of having a greater sense of autonomy:

Reduced stress:

When we have control over our time and energy, we are able to reduce stress and manage our workload more effectively. We can set realistic goals and prioritize our tasks, which can help us feel more in control and less overwhelmed. This can also lead to improved mental health and overall well-being.

Improved productivity:

Having autonomy over our time and energy can also lead to improved productivity. When we have the freedom to work on our own terms, we are able to focus more deeply and get more done in less time. We can also schedule our work around our natural rhythms and energy levels, which can help us stay motivated and engaged.

Greater sense of fulfilment:

When we have autonomy over our time and energy, we are able to pursue the things that are most important to us. This can lead to a greater sense of fulfilment and purpose in our lives. We can focus on our passions and interests, which can bring us joy and a sense of accomplishment.

More meaningful relationships:

Having autonomy over our time and energy can also lead to more meaningful relationships. When we can prioritize our time and energy in a way that feels authentic to us, we are better able to connect with others on a deeper level. We can be more present in our relationships and show up as our authentic selves.

Increased creativity:

Autonomy over our time and energy can also lead to increased creativity. When we have the freedom to explore our passions and interests, we are able to tap into our creative potential and come up with new ideas and solutions. We can also take risks and try new things, which can help us grow and develop as individuals.

When we are single, we have the freedom to pursue our personal goals and aspirations without the constraints of a romantic relationship. This can be a wonderful opportunity to focus on our own growth and development. Here are some of the ways being single can provide opportunities to achieve personal goals and aspirations:

Time and energy:

When we are single, we often have more time and energy to dedicate to our personal goals and aspirations. We don't have to worry about scheduling around someone else's needs or compromising our own time and energy. This means we can focus on what's most important to us and work towards our goals without distraction.

Financial independence:

Being single also means we have more financial independence. We are in control of our own finances and can make decisions about how to spend our money. This can provide us with the resources we need to pursue our personal goals and aspirations, whether that's investing in education, starting a business, or pursuing a hobby.

Greater flexibility:

Being single also provides greater flexibility in terms of how we live our lives. We can make decisions about where we want to live, how we want to spend our time, and what we want to do without having to consider the needs or desires of a partner. This can be especially helpful when pursuing personal goals and aspirations that require a certain level of flexibility or mobility.

Increased self-awareness:

Being single can also provide an opportunity for increased self-awareness. When we are not in a relationship, we have more time to reflect on our own values, beliefs, and priorities. This can help us gain clarity about what we truly want out of life and what steps we need to take to achieve our goals and aspirations.

More support:

Finally, being single does not mean we have to go it alone. In fact, being single can provide us with more opportunities for support from friends, family, and the community. We can build a support network of people who share our values and aspirations, and who can provide encouragement, guidance, and accountability as we work towards our goals.

Chapter 6

The Power of Alone Time

In our busy, fast-paced lives, it can be easy to get caught up in the constant noise and distractions of the world around us. But taking time to be alone with ourselves and our thoughts can be incredibly beneficial for our mental, emotional, and even physical well-being. Here are some of the reasons why alone time and solitude are so important:

Self-reflection:

One of the most important reasons to spend time alone is for self-reflection. When we are alone, we have the opportunity to reflect on our thoughts, feelings, and experiences without the distractions of other people or the outside world. This can help us gain a better understanding of ourselves, our values, and our priorities, and can help us make more intentional choices about how we want to live our lives.

Mental and emotional health:

Alone time and solitude can also be beneficial for our mental and emotional health. It can provide a sense of calm and quiet that is often difficult to find in our busy lives. Spending time alone can help us reduce stress, anxiety, and depression, and can help us recharge and renew our energy.

Creativity:

Alone time and solitude can also be incredibly beneficial for creativity. When we are alone, we have the space to let our minds wander and explore new ideas and possibilities. This can be especially helpful for creative pursuits like writing, art, or music, where having the freedom to experiment and take risks can lead to new and exciting breakthroughs.

Independence:

Spending time alone can also help us develop a greater sense of independence. When we are alone, we are responsible for our own needs and decisions, which can help us build confidence and self-reliance. This can be especially important for young people who are still figuring out who they are and what they want in life.

Connection:

Finally, paradoxically, alone time and solitude can actually help us feel more connected to others. When we take the time to reflect on our own thoughts and experiences, we often gain a deeper understanding and empathy for the experiences of others. This can help us build stronger, more authentic relationships with the people around us.

First and foremost, let's define what we mean by "recharge and reflect." When we talk about recharging, we mean taking time to rest and rejuvenate our minds and bodies. This could mean anything from taking a nap, going for a walk, or simply sitting quietly and doing nothing for a while. Reflection, on the other hand, is the act of thinking deeply about our thoughts, feelings, and experiences. It's a time for introspection, self-awareness, and growth.

So, why is it important to be able to recharge and reflect without the distractions of a romantic partner? Here are a few reasons.

It allows us to focus on ourselves:

When we're in a romantic relationship, it's natural to prioritize our partner's needs and wants. We want to spend time with them, make them happy, and take care of them. While these are all important things to do, it's also important to take care of ourselves. Taking time to recharge and reflect allows us to focus on our own needs and wants, and to prioritize our own well-being.

It helps us to be more self-aware:

When we're alone, we have the opportunity to be more self-aware. We can reflect on our thoughts, feelings, and behaviours without the influence of another person. This can help us to better understand ourselves, our strengths and weaknesses, and our patterns of behaviour. Being self-aware can also help us to make better decisions and to have more fulfilling relationships in the future.

It promotes personal growth:

When we take time to recharge and reflect, we give ourselves the opportunity to grow and develop as individuals. We can set goals for ourselves, work on personal projects, or simply learn new things. This can help us to become more confident, independent, and fulfilled in our lives.

Of course, it's important to note that being in a romantic relationship can also have many benefits. We can learn from our partners, grow together, and experience love and intimacy. However, it's also important to have a balance between being with another person and being alone.

So, how can we create the space to recharge and reflect without the distractions of a romantic partner? Here are a few ideas:

Schedule alone time:

Make a point to schedule alone time into your calendar. This could be a few hours each week, or an entire weekend every month. Whatever works for you, make sure to prioritize this time and stick to it.

Find a quiet space:

Choose a quiet space where you can be alone and undisturbed. This could be a room in your house, a park, or a quiet café. Wherever you choose, make sure it's a place where you feel comfortable and relaxed.

Practice mindfulness:

Use mindfulness techniques to help you stay present and focused during your alone time. This could include meditation, deep breathing, or simply paying attention to your surroundings. By practising mindfulness, you can quiet your mind and fully immerse yourself in the present moment.

In our society, we often place a lot of emphasis on socializing and being around other people. While having strong social connections is certainly important, it's also valuable to be able to enjoy our own company and find fulfilment in solitary pursuits. Here are a few reasons why:

It promotes self-awareness.

When we spend time alone, we have the opportunity to reflect on our thoughts, feelings, and experiences. This can help us to become more self-aware and understand ourselves on a deeper level. When we know ourselves better, we can make better decisions and have more fulfilling relationships.

It allows us to pursue our own interests.

When we're alone, we can pursue our own interests without worrying about the opinions or expectations of others. We can read a book, take a walk, learn a new skill, or simply relax and do nothing. By doing things that we enjoy, we can increase our sense of fulfilment and happiness.

It helps us to recharge.

Spending time alone can be a great way to recharge our batteries. When we're constantly around other people, we may feel drained or overwhelmed. Taking time for ourselves can help us to feel more refreshed and energized.

So, how can we learn to enjoy our own company and find fulfilment in solitary pursuits? Here are a few ideas:

Practice mindfulness.

Mindfulness is the practice of being present and fully engaged in the moment. When we're alone, we can use mindfulness techniques to stay present and focused on our experiences. This can help us to appreciate the little things in life and find joy in simple pleasures.

Engage in hobbies and interests.

Think about the things that you enjoy doing and make time for them. Whether it's reading, writing, painting, or playing music, find ways to pursue your interests and passions. This can help you to feel fulfilled and happy, even when you're alone.

Try new things.

Spending time alone can be a great opportunity to try new things and step out of your comfort zone. Take a class, try a new hobby, or explore a new part of town.

Conclusion

Being single is often seen as a negative state, and many people feel pressure to be in a relationship. However, being single can be a positive and empowering choice. Here are a few conclusions we can draw about being single:

It's a time for self-discovery.

When we're single, we have the opportunity to focus on ourselves and our own personal growth. We can take the time to explore our interests and passions and figure out what we truly want in life. This can help us to become more self-aware and confident, and ultimately lead to more fulfilling relationships in the future.

It's a time for independence.

Being single allows us to be independent and make our own choices without the influence of a partner. We can travel, take risks, and try new things without worrying about the opinions or expectations of someone else. This can be incredibly liberating and empowering.

It's a time for building strong friendships.

When we're single, we often have more time and energy to devote to our friendships. We can build deep, meaningful connections with other people and create a strong support network. This can be especially important during difficult times and can ultimately lead to more fulfilling relationships in the future.

It's not a reflection of our worth.

Being single does not define our worth as individuals. We are valuable and worthy of love and respect regardless of our relationship status. We should never feel pressured to be in a relationship or feel like being single makes us less valuable or desirable.

It can be a choice.

Lastly, it's important to remember that being single can be a choice. We don't need to be in a relationship to be happy or fulfilled. If we choose to be single, we can embrace it and enjoy all the benefits that come with it.

Contents

Printed by Libri Plureos GmbH in Hamburg,
Germany